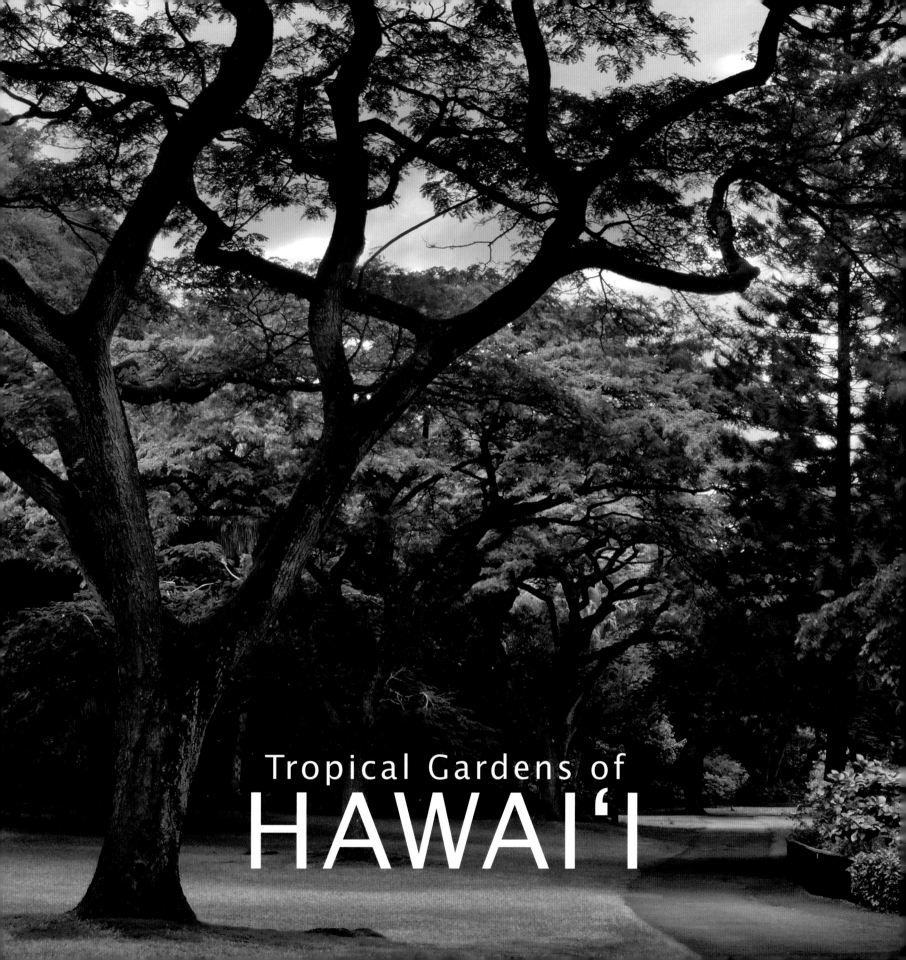

Tropical Gardens of
HAWAI'I

Tropical Gardens of Hawai'i

David Leaser

MUTUAL PUBLISHING

ISBN-10: 1-56647-862-6
ISBN-13: 978-1-56647-862-5

Library of Congress Cataloging-in-Publication Data

Leaser, David.
  Tropical gardens of Hawai'i / David Leaser.
      p. cm.
  Includes bibliographical references and index.
  ISBN 1-56647-862-6 (hardcover : alk. paper)
  1. Gardens--Hawaii. 2. Gardens--Hawaii--Pictorial works.
I. Title.
  SB466.U6L423 2008
  712.09969--dc22
                                        2008004605

Image on page 114, left © Dole Plantation
Image on page 120, bottom right © Honolulu Botanical
    Gardens
All other images © David Leaser
Front cover: Dole Plantation
Page 1: Waimea Valley on O'ahu's famous North Shore.
Frontispiece: Ho'omaluhia Botanical Garden in
    Kāne'ohe on the Island of O'ahu.
Page 6: A native *Hibiscus arnottianus*.
Page 192: Ho'omaluhia Botanical Garden at sunrise.

Design by David Leaser

First Printing, April 2008

Mutual Publishing, LLC
1215 Center Street, Suite 210
Honolulu, HI 96816
Ph: 808-732-1709 / Fax: 808-734-4094
E:mail: info@mutualpublishing.com
www.mutualpublishing.com

Printed in Taiwan

Contents

Foreword

Upon arriving in Hawai'i in 1950, I found that Foster Garden was the sole botanical garden in the Islands. As master planner for the city's park system, I was able to locate funds for needed improvements to the aging garden. Dr. Harold Lyon, then director of the garden and holder of a highly responsible position with the Hawaiian Sugar Planters' Association, had developed a far-sighted scheme to establish a comprehensive botanical garden system. Public meetings created strong public support, but unfortunately Dr. Lyon died before firm action could be taken. His foresight, however, was not for naught. His long-range plan was pursued by a committee of dedicated influential citizens and the result was the creation of the National Tropical Botanical Garden on Kaua'i.

To my complete surprise, I was notified on the day of Dr. Lyon's death in 1957 that I was now the director of Foster Botanical Garden, a position arranged by Dr. Lyon himself prior to his passing.

Beginning in 1957, a major influence in the formative years of my professional life was my association for five years with the internationally known Dr. Joseph C. Rock. His work on the Hawaiian flora is monumental. He propelled me into the world of serious botanical collecting, specifically the native endangered flora.

The following thirty-three years were almost violently action-packed. I was struck by the incredible opportunity of expanding the garden system to include areas of other growing environments. We had the historical lowland, warm Foster Garden and a developing cool, moist site in Wahiawā. We soon acquired two hundred-acre Koko Crater, the perfect site for a collection of drought-tolerant species.

Through the action of the U.S. Army Corps of Engineers, a magnificent four hundred-acre site backed by almost vertical cliffs of the Ko'olau mountain range rising to three thousand feet, was developed as the Ho`omaluhia Botanical Garden, a repository of tropical warm, wetland species.

All that remained was the locating of an on-shore, salt wind site to receive a collection of tropical strand species. I did not manage to realize that.

I retired (my wife says I "only re-treaded") at the end of 1989, but I am still active as a volunteer. I am delighted with the young people who are now on the Board of the Friends of Honolulu Botanical Gardens and the realization that my passions as well as a higher level of community service will be realized by these wonderful young people. It's really my time to retire.

Today, Hawai'i's botanical gardens and native forests are a precious, living museum, a treasure of tropical plants for science, conservation, learning, and recreation. Many emphasize the rare and endangered Hawaiian flora as well as similar species from the tropical parts of the globe, species that have found the Islands a conservation refuge; others emphasize more ornamental species and hybrids.

David Leaser has captured the spirit and fact of Hawai`i's gardens both visually through his fine photography and through his clear writing. It is a work long overdue. I am proud to be even a small part of his accomplishment.

Aloha and Mahalo nui loa,
Paul R. Weissich
Director Emeritus, Honolulu Botanical Gardens

Introduction

If God were designing the Garden of Eden today, surely He would consider a lush tropical place with jagged green mountains, swaying coconut palms, and fresh air subtly scented with the perfume of exotic flowers. This is Hawai'i, a place that to many symbolizes the essence of the tropics.

But it wasn't always that way. Located near the Tropic of Cancer, the Hawaiian Islands are halfway between California and Japan, more than three thousand miles from any continent. When they arose from the sea millions of years ago, the Hawaiian Islands were a barren wasteland, devoid of any living things. Because they were not attached to any land mass, all of Hawai'i's plants and animals had to arrive by chance, carried at first by birds, insects, the tradewinds, and the sea. In time, these colonists evolved to form Hawai'i's first endemic species and genera. But, aside from the native hibiscus, the showy flowers of other plants like the plumeria, orchid, and ginger would come much later, introduced by American and European settlers.

Left: A tropical display garden greets visitors to the National Tropical Botanical Garden's visitor center in Po'ipū on the island of Kaua'i. Bromeliads, palms, ferns and gingers line pathways which lead to a plantation-style visitors' center.

More than 1,500 years ago, Polynesians arrived on the Islands, and with them the plants that defined their culture. An estimated twenty-six species were introduced to provide food, shelter, tools, medicine, and textiles. Coconut palms, bananas, sweet potatoes, breadfruit, and the now-ubiquitous Hawaiian ti were among the plants to arrive in Polynesian canoes.

By the mid-nineteenth century, Honolulu had grown into a bustling harbor town with little urban planning. Ramshackle houses lined narrow, dusty streets.

But that was all about to change. Shortly after he arrived on December 28, 1850, William Hillebrand, a physician by trade, set out to change the landscape in the emerging metropolis, importing many of the exotic flowering trees that now characterize the Islands.

Born and raised in Germany, Hillebrand developed an interest in botany and a wanderlust for the tropics at an early age. After living in Australia, the Philippines, and San Francisco, Hillebrand arrived in Honolulu aboard the barque *Elizabeth* and was quickly accepted into the social circles of the Hawaiian ali'i, or royalty. Named chief physician of the new Queen's Hospital and personal physician

Opposite: Waimea Valley on O'ahu's famed North Shore displays a replica of the eating pavilions used by early Hawaiians. The site is planted with ti (*Cordyline fruticosa*) and hala (*Pandanus tectorius*) used by early settlers.

Above: The jagged Ko'olau Mountains on the windward coast of O'ahu provide a spectacular backdrop for the four hundred-acre Ho'omaluhia Botanical Garden. Native plants, including koa (*Acacia koa*), share the landscape with introduced species from around the tropical world.

to King Kamehameha V, Hillebrand was soon commissioned by the Kingdom of Hawai'i to seek cures for leprosy, import beneficial animals and plants, and find overseas sources of labor for sugar plantations. Hillebrand recruited the first wave of Portuguese immigrants to the Islands in 1877.

Hillebrand's passion for plants and botany has made, perhaps, his most lasting impact on the Hawaiian Islands. Hillebrand's influence with the royal family led to the establishment of Hawai'i's first nursery on thirty acres of land in Waikahalulu, leased from Queen Kalama. At the Queen's Hospital in Honolulu, two bombax trees (*Pseudobombax ellipticum*) he planted still grace the grounds.

Dr. Hillebrand's strong friendship with the era's leading botanists like Sir William Hooker, director of Kew Gardens in London, and his incessant requests for new plants led to an influx of beneficial and ornamental species to the Islands. At every opportunity, Hillebrand persuaded

Opposite: clockwise from top left: Brilliant red flowers of the royal poinciana tree (*Delonix regia*), native to Madagascar; Singapore plumerias (*Plumeria obtusa*) grow throughout the Islands; oleanders (*Nerium oleander*) from Africa flourish in dry areas around the Islands. **Right:** An Australian flame tree (*Brachychiton acerifolius*) brightens the dense greenery at Ho'omaluhia Botanical Garden.

his friends, even Queen Emma, to transport miniature greenhouses, called Wardian cases, around the globe, to collect specimens.

His efforts paid off, and many of the exotic plants that now beautify Hawai'i's landscape can be traced to his persistence. From the shower trees (*Cassia* species) and royal poincianas (*Delonix regia*) to the showy orchids, gingers, jasmines, and bromeliads, the impact Hillebrand's imports made on Hawai'i's present-day landscape cannot be overstated.

During his visit to Hawai'i in 1866, Mark Twain wrote of Honolulu's beautiful shade trees and dense thickets of flowers. In only sixteen years, Hillebrand had realized his dream to transform the dusty streets of Honolulu into the canopied roadways we see today.

Among the plethora of Hillebrand's botanical imports, perhaps the most memorable is one of Hawai'i's most beloved, the frangipani-scented plumeria. The plumeria lei is as much a symbol of Hawai'i as is Diamond Head.

Hillebrand was equally interested in promoting Hawai'i's flora abroad. His expeditions around the Islands led to the discovery and classification of a great many

Opposite: Originally established in 1918 by the Hawaiian Sugar Planters' Association as a watershed restoration project, Lyon Arboretum's two hundred-acre site on O'ahu features an extensive collection of tropical plants, many of which have naturalized in the garden's mountainous terrain.

Above: Stilt palms (*Verschaffeltia splendida*) and majesty palms (*Ravenea rivulis*) line a paved lane at Ho'omaluhia Botanical Garden in Kāne'ohe.

Above: The Lāwaʻi Stream cuts through Allerton Garden on the island of Kauaʻi before it empties into the Pacific Ocean.
Opposite: A manmade stream flows from behind a Japanese tea house at the University of Hawaiʻi's Japanese garden.

plants, later documented in his published work on the subject. He tirelessly promoted economically important Hawaiian plants, including koa as an alternative to mahogany.

When he departed Hawai'i in 1871, William Hillebrand left behind a legacy which is a significant part of the fabric of Hawai'i's culture today. Two years after his death from tuberculosis in 1886, Hillebrand's *Flora of the Hawaiian Islands*, a comprehensive tome on the plant life of Hawai'i, was published. It remains an important treatise on Hawai'i's endemic plants.

Hillebrand's estate was sold to Thomas and Mary Foster in 1880. The Fosters soon built a large Victorian home on the five-acre parcel, replacing the original Hillebrand house. Mary Foster, who was part-Hawaiian, renovated the garden and installed a canal system to irrigate the plants. But after her husband died in 1889, Foster abandoned the property to live with her sister. She later returned and restored the property to its former glory, adding new plants and trees. Perhaps her most memorable contribution is also one of the garden's most famous: a bo tree (*Ficus religiosa*) descended from the famous tree where Buddha received enlightenment in India.

In the early twentieth century, Mary Foster solicited the help of botanist Harold Lyon to restore the garden. Lyon had recently arrived from Minnesota to work for the Hawaiian Sugar Planters' Association, researching sugar cane diseases and importing plants to reforest the watershed that was destroyed by grazing cattle. Foster leased two acres of the garden to the association to develop a plant nursery.

When she died in 1930 at the age of eighty-six, Mary Foster bequeathed the property to the City of Honolulu with the provision it remain as a public garden. In 1931, the garden opened its doors as Foster Park, Hawai'i's first botanical garden. With Harold Lyon as its first director, the garden continued to improve and increase in size with donations of neighboring parcels. Lyon cleared overgrown areas, installed an irrigation system and built a glasshouse to house an impressive collection of orchids. Now called

Opposite: clockwise from left: A sealing wax palm (*Cyrtostachys renda*) at Nani Mau Gardens on the Big Island; a pigtail anthurium (*Anthurium scherzerianum*) at Kula Botanical Garden on Maui; a red-flowering banana (*Musa coccinea*).
Right: Tropical foliage surrounds a manmade pond at the Dole Plantation in central O'ahu. The Dole Plantation's botanical garden includes a large collection of bromeliads, gingers, and hibiscus hybrids.

Foster Botanical Garden, the location remains the flagship garden of the Honolulu Botanical Gardens.

Harold Lyon died in 1957 and was succeeded by Paul R. Weissich, a landscape architect from California. Weissich continued to improve Foster Botanical Garden, adding an economic garden, a glen with prehistoric plants and the Harold L. Lyon Orchid Garden. But that was just the beginning for Weissich. Under his direction, a massive expansion was about to begin. Weissich developed a master plan for future growth that included a network of public gardens. During his tenure, Honolulu Botanical Gardens expanded to include a network of gardens encompassing more than four hundred acres. Paul Weissich could be considered the father of the modern-day Honolulu Botanical Garden system.

Left: Koko Crater Botanical Garden on Oʻahu is home to an extensive collection of dryland species, including the octopus cactus (*Rathbunia alamosensis*).
Opposite: clockwise from left: a silver vase bromeliad (*Aechmea fasciata*); a variegated canna hybrid; a hybrid hibiscus; *Heliconia chartacea 'Sexy Pink'*; a fragrant *Gardenia thunbergii*; a hybrid heliconia.

Opposite: from far left: Introduced from Mexico, the plumeria has become the unofficial botanical symbol of Hawai'i; an exotic *Amherstia nobilis* tree blooms at Lyon Arboretum.
Above: A restored plantation-era cottage at the National Tropical Botanical Garden's south shore location on the island of Kaua'i houses the visitors' center and gift shop. The cottage is surrounded by ten acres of gardens featuring native species, fruit trees, and a wide variety of ornamental trees and shrubs.

Throughout the Islands, similar pioneers were developing their own botanical gardens, many for private use. Today, the Islands hold a treasure trove of magnificent gardens, each with a unique theme. From Kaua'i's Allerton Garden, famously depicted in *Jurassic Park*, to the Big Island's Hawai'i Tropical Botanical Garden, each contributes to the beauty of the Islands and offers visitors a glimpse of the tropical wonders from around the globe.

From its humble beginnings as a volcanic outcrop devoid of vegetation, Hawai'i is now home to a great rarity of endangered flora. More than 90% of the native terrestrial plants are found only in the Hawaiian Islands, the highest level of endemism in the world. With the added beauty of more than a century of introductions, Hawai'i is truly a tropical paradise beyond compare.

Left: A blue variety of a native loulu palm (*Pritchardia hillebrandii*) at Ho'omaluhia Botanical Garden on O'ahu.
Opposite: clockwise from top left: Hau; swiss cheese plant (*Monstera deliciosa*) are common in Hawai'i's landscape; anthuriums bloom throughout the Islands.

Above: Stone steps at Waimea Valley lead into a dense jungle of peace lilies (*Spathyphyllum wallisii*) and assorted vines.
Opposite: Native to Madagascar, brilliant orange royal poinciana trees (*Delonix regia*) grow well in Hawai'i's dry leeward gardens.

Gardens of Kaua'i

Allerton Garden

In the Lāwa'i Valley on Kaua'i's west coast, purple bougainvillea cascades down the volcanic slopes to a verdant valley below. The valley is a former retreat of Queen Emma, wife of King Kamehameha IV, whose passion for exotic plants endures in what is now one of the island's most beautiful spots.

In the nineteenth century, King Kamehameha III redistributed land during the Great Māhele, allowing chiefs and commoners to acquire and own property. In 1848, Lāwa'i Valley was granted to James Young Kanehoa, son of John Young, an advisor to Hawai'i's King Kamehameha I. Upon his death, Kanehoa willed his land to his niece, Queen Emma. Upon the death of her husband and young son, the queen retreated to Lāwa'i, where she planted rose apples, mangoes, bamboo, and the purple bougainvillea that now bears her name.

In 1886, the neighboring McBryde family purchased the land from Queen Emma to plant taro and rice. A decade

Left: Threatened sea turtles nest on a pristine beach at Allerton Garden. A footbridge spans the Lāwa'i Stream that bisects the garden.

Above: clockwise from top left: Moreton Bay fig trees (*Ficus macrophylla*), planted in the 1940s, served as a backdrop for the movie *Jurassic Park*; the Allerton residence, built in 1938; the entrance to the tropical fruit orchard; a lotus pond occupies the spot which once held an ancient Hawaiian fishpond.
Opposite: A statue of the Greek goddess Diana stands on a pedestal overlooking a reflecting pool and lattice pavilion.

later, Alexander McBryde took up residence on the property, planting palms, gingers, plumerias, and ferns throughout the valley.

In 1938, Alexander McBryde sold the lower half of the valley to Robert Allerton, a wealthy son of a *Mayflower* descendant. The Allerton family had made their fortune in Chicago, investing in real estate, cattle, and banking, but Robert was captivated by the Lāwa'i Valley and made it his summer home. Here, with his adopted son John, Allerton was able to exercise his passion for landscape architecture, creating a series of garden rooms with gazebos, water features, and statuary on the eighty-acre plot. The Allertons continued in the tradition of Queen Emma and Alexander McBryde, adding to the growing plant collection. Lāwa'i Kai became an organized, but jungled valley divided by a lazy stream that reaches to a secluded beach. Upon his death in 1964, Robert Allerton bequeathed the estate to his son, who continued to maintain the property with their trusted gardener, Hideo Teshima. After John's death in the 1980s, the Allerton Gardens Trust was established, and the garden is now managed by the National Tropical Botanical Garden.

Today, the garden is a vision of unparalled beauty and a piece of Kaua'i's history. From the historic plantings of Queen Emma to the impressive collections of heliconias, shower trees, bamboos, and plumerias, the site has become a structured tropical Arcadia, where nearly every plant was introduced but creates a sense of an ordered, natural rainforest. Visitors will see towering talipot palms, thunbergia vines, and night-blooming cereus clinging to volcanic hillsides. Tour guides sometimes allow visitors to wander into the Victory Garden, planted during World War II, to sample a lychee or starfruit.

Hollywood has taken note of this pristine location, filming movies and television shows in the valley. Visitors will quickly identify the Moreton Bay fig trees featured in *Jurassic Park* and the garden's secluded beach used in *South Pacific.*

Today, more than a century after Queen Emma planted her first bouganvillea, Allerton Garden remains a sublime botanical retreat.

Opposite: Coconut palms *(Cocos nucifera)* grow along the Lāwaʻi Stream, which flows through the garden.
Above: clockwise from left: Bouganvillea, planted by Queen Emma in the nineteenth Century, still clings to the hillsides in the garden; an old red sugar cane pumphouse is surrounded by vegetables and tropical plants; the Lāwaʻi Stream flows to the sea.

Limahuli Garden and Preserve

At the base of Makana Mountain on Kaua'i's northern coast, a verdant tropical valley has been transformed into a botanical garden that overlooks the Pacific Ocean. Called *Limahuli,* which means "turning hands," the garden is a lasting tribute to early Hawaiians who carved the valley into a series of volcanic stone terraces. Here, for hundreds of years, taro and sweet potato provided sustenance to the local Hawaiian village.

After the Great Māhele of 1848, King Kamehameha III's decree to divide the islands into parcels, the land was sold and converted to a cattle farm. After more than a century of grazing, the land was stripped of any remaining native species and reforested with faster-growing non-native trees.

In 1967, Limahuli Valley was assigned to Juliet Rice Wichman, a member of the Hui Kū'ai 'Āina O Hā'ena, an association that had acquired the entire valley in 1875. Recognizing the need to preserve Hawai'i's remaining native plants,

Left: Makana Mountain towers over ancient taro terraces on Kaua'i's north coast. The mountain is known by visitors as "Bali Hai" because of its representation in the movie *South Pacific.*

Wichman began to restore the valley to its original splendor. After adding service roads, she cleared a majority of the non-native plants and restored the lava terraces. Upon her death in 1976, Wichman donated the lower portion of the valley, by then called Limahuli Garden, to the National Tropical Botanical Garden, leaving the remaining 985 acres to her grandson, Chipper, who gave the land to the National Botanical Garden to create the Limahuli Garden and Preserve.

In 1995, the garden opened to the public and was quickly recognized by the American Horticultural Society with its "Best Natural Botanical Garden" designation for demonstrating "best sound environmental practices of water, soil, and rare native plant conservation in an overall garden design."

Today, the garden welcomes visitors to step back in time to see an agricultural preserve that looks much like it did in ancient times. Limahuli Stream, with its eight hundred-foot waterfall, courses through the valley past lava terraces before entering the ocean.

Left: Limahuli Stream traverses the garden.
Opposite: clockwise from left: A rare endemic St. John's hibiscus (*Hibiscus kokio subsp. saintjohnianus*); a bromeliad grows in lava rock; a native koa (*Acacia koa*).

Above: clockwise from top left: Moss-covered stones cross Lāwaʻi Stream; a tall kukui tree (*Aleurites moluccana*); a native ʻilima (*Sida fallax*); tree roots cling to lava rock.
Opposite: The pinwheel flower of the Tahitian gardenia (*Gardenia tatiensis*).

The Hawaiian ethnobotanical collection includes plants cultivated by early Hawaiians, such as taro, sweet potato, bananas, and sugar cane.

The garden also pays homage to plantation-era plants, including Hawai'i's emblematic plumeria and a variety of gingers and heliconias.

But it's the native plant collection that may be the most important. The garden focuses on species from northwestern Kaua'i and includes specimens of rare and endangered species that are on the verge of extinction. A native palm, *Pritchardia limahuliensis,* is found only in Limahuli Valley. The odd-looking *Brighamia insignis,* or ālula, which looks like a cabbage on a stick, is found only on the sea cliffs of the neighboring Nā Pali coastline. Other plants are so rare they have almost been lost to time. Kaua'i's native hibiscus, *Hibiscus waimeae subsp. hannerae,* or koki'o ke'oke'o, was thought extinct until it was rediscovered in the back of the valley.

Today, Limahuli Valley houses a research center and preserve with a seventeen-acre garden for visitors. With panoramic views of emerald green peaks and azure waters, the garden is a perfect place to experience the beauty of Kaua'i's North Shore.

Opposite: An endemic hibiscus (*Hibiscus kokio*).
Above: A lone hala, also called screwpine (*Pandanus tectorius*), shades a bench overlooking Kaua'i's north coast.

McBryde Garden

Kauaʻi, Hawaiʻi's oldest island has a well-deserved reputation as the Garden Isle of Hawaiʻi. With its jagged-peaked mountains, verdant valleys, and pristine waters, Kauaʻi is a tropical paradise of extreme diversity. The island boasts the largest canyon in the Pacific, picturesque coastlines, and the wettest spot on earth; Kauaʻi's interior receives more than five hundred inches of rain each year.

In such a place, the National Tropical Botanical Garden was born when, in 1970, a portion of the Lāwaʻi Valley was purchased by a young non-profit organization to serve as a botanical garden, propagation facility, and research center. The valley had recently been used as a sugar plantation, with a history that dates back to the days of Hawaiian royalty. Once a retreat for Queen Emma, wife of King Kamehameha IV, the land was purchased by Judge Duncan McBryde, a prospective sugar farmer in 1886. There, McBryde installed a railway, water pumping stations, and aqueducts to develop the land into what was to become the McBryde Sugar Company.

Left: Tangled vines dangle from a tree over the main drive that loops the garden.

Today, the 252-acre garden and reserve is open to visitors to explore what has matured into one of Hawai'i's finest botanical gardens. A visitors' center, housed in a 1930s-era sugar plantation home, is surrounded by ten acres of display gardens, showcasing plumerias, bromeliads, tropical fruits, and native Hawaiian plants. From there, visitors board a shuttle van for a two-mile tour into the Lāwa'i Valley to visit McBryde or neighboring Allerton Garden. The road into the valley is narrow, traversing old train trestles that have been retrofitted for the journey. Once inside the garden, visitors disembark to explore the extensive plantings of palms, flowering trees, and tropical plants.

The garden includes a Hawaiian native garden with plantings of native screwpine, or hala (*Pandanus tectorius*), sandalwoods (*Santalum ellipticum*), and other more rare endemic plants. The garden displays an impressive collection of several rare species of Hawai'i's only native palm genus, *Pritchardia*. Colorful natives, including the white *Hibiscus waimeae* and and yellow 'ilima (*Sida fallax*) add a touch of color to the garden,

Opposite: clockwise from far left: The palm garden; fruit of a native loulu (*Pritchardia*) palm; fruit of the Vahane palm (*Pelagodoxa henryana*).
Right: The frond of *Licuala orbicularis*.

and *Gardenia brighamii*, one of Hawai'i's native gardenias, adds a spicy fragrance to the air.

Called canoe plants, early Polynesian introductions grow throughout the valley, including a special garden showing visitors their early uses. Noni (*Morinda citrifolia*), introduced by the Polynesians, and used for dye and medicinal purposes, is today being investigated as a potential remedy for tuberculosis and cancer. Noni juice is an iconic remedy for everything from fatigue to insomnia. Kukui (*Aleurites moluccana*) trees, with their whitish leaves, were valued for their seeds which were pressed to produce oil for lamps. Sweet potato and taro were important food sources, and every part of the now ubiquitous coconut palm was used by Hawai'i's first settlers.

The garden displays a large collection of brilliantly colored gingers, heliconias, and birds of paradise, all members of the

Left: The palm path, lined with mondo grass, leads to a foot bridge across a creek. Epiphytic orchids grow in the trees.
Opposite: clockwise from top left: The colorful fruit and crownshaft of the orange collar palm (*Areca vestiaria*); the windowed leaf of *Reinhardtia gracilis*; cacao (*Theobroma cacao*) grows on the garden's Spice Walk; a banyan tree provides a home for various epiphytic plants; bromeliads naturalize on a hillside; Red ginger (*Alpinia purpurata*) brighten a densely vegetated area of the garden.

Above: Loulu palms (*Pritchardia remota*), native to the neighboring island of Nihoa.
Opposite: Canopied paths make it easy to explore the garden.

botanical order *Zingiberales*. ʻĀwapuhi, or shampoo ginger, was introduced by early Polynesians and used as a shampoo and hair conditioner.

The garden's spice walk offers visitors a special treat. Chocolate trees (*Theobroma cacao*), pepper plants (*Piper nigrum*), allspice trees (*Pimenta dioica*) and vanilla vines (*Vanilla planifolia*), with their fragrant white orchid flowers, are standouts.

A bamboo bridge across the Lāwaʻi Stream leads to the Reading Palm Walk, a display of rare and unusual palms, including the near-extinct Vahane palm (*Pelagodoxa henryana*) from the Marquesas Islands. Colorful flowering plants, like the red jade vine (*Mucuna bennettii*) and the pagoda plant (*Clerodendrum paniculatum*) brighten the densely planted walkway.

In less than four decades, McBryde Garden has become a botanical treasure of tropical flora for visitors and an important research and propagation center, preserving these botanical wonders for future generations.

Gardens of the Big Island

'Akaka Falls State Park

'Akaka Falls State Park offers a dramatic backdrop few other gardens can provide. Plunging more than four hundred feet into a gorge, 'Akaka Falls is the star of the garden, providing the perfect foil for the dense greenery of this jungle-like park. Hawaiian legend says the waterfall was created by the adulterous god, 'Akaka. After his wife returned home to discover his infidelity, 'Akaka fled the scene, slipping on the edge of the canyon and plunging to the valley below.

Just north of Hilo, this garden is a tropical paradise, with paths winding through sixty-four densely vegetated acres. Paved steps lead down a steep ravine to a loop around the garden, which meanders for nearly a half mile past stands of bamboo, ferns, gingers, hibiscus, and heliconias. Throughout the garden, tropical plants have naturalized, giving the park an untamed quality. Impatiens grow out of crusted lava, and ferns cling to the cliffs that border the garden. Tree roots break out of the garden and provide secure pockets for small understorey plants. And tropical

Left: Paved paths lead through a thick jungle-like garden to 'Akaka Falls.

vines snake through the trees seeking the sun at the top of the canopy. As you walk through the garden, you are soon rewarded with the crashing sounds of water, followed by unobstructed views of two waterfalls, the largest of which is 'Akaka. Further down the path, smaller Kahuna Falls cascades one hundred feet down the hill to Kolekole Stream, surrounded by kukui nut trees and a lush, green landscape. Plan to spend at least an hour at 'Akaka Falls State Park to enjoy its tranquility. Wooden picnic tables and restroom facilities make this park a perfect stop for a picnic in paradise.

Opposite: clockwise from top left: A pink-fruiting banana (*Musa velutina*); vines climb the trees throughout the park; mosses grow in the moist, tropical air; palm flowers emerge from *Pinanga kuhlii*; white flowers of the skyflower vine (*Thunbergia grandiflora*); mosses appear to consume a striped bamboo (*Bambusa vulgaris vittata*).
Right: 'Akaka Falls plunges four hundred feet to a stream that leads to the Hāmākua Coast.

Amy B.H. Greenwell Ethnobotanical Garden

Polynesians brought nearly thirty plants with them when they settled the Hawaiian Islands. From important food crops to plants used for timber and daily sustenance, these plants helped Hawai'i's first settlers develop their culture. Throughout the Islands, early Hawaiians developed sophisticated agriculture and horticulture skills, planting farms and harvesting the bounty. In the hills above the Kona coastline on the Big Island of Hawai'i, Hawaiian farmers created more than fifty square miles of farmland out of the fallow, volcanic slopes. Here they planted taro, sweet potatoes, ti, and other crops.

In Captain Cook, about twelve miles south of Kailua-Kona on the Big Island of Hawai'i, a small slice of history in the form of a fifteen-acre botanical garden was donated by Amy B.H. Greenwell to the Bishop Museum in 1974. Remnants of prehistoric agricultural systems are scattered throughout the garden, the most prominent of which are the kuaiwi, long stone ridges that mark the boundaries for the various crops.

Left: Hala (*Pandanus tectorius*) and ti plants (*Cordyline fruticosa*) grow in the volcanic soil of South Kona.

The garden is divided into the four vegetation zones used by early Hawaiians in the region. The Coastal Zone features plants from the seashore, including naupaka, hau, coconut, and kou. The Lowland Dry Forest displays native shrubs and trees from the dry, barren areas of West Hawai'i. Many of these plants are nearly extinct, and the garden acts as a resource for preservation. The Agricultural Zone features bananas, sugarcane, taro, and other food crops; and the Upland Forest displays hibiscus, hau, and hardwoods like koa, a favored wood for building early canoes.

Plan to spend an hour to enjoy the history and significance that early botany and agriculture played in the settlement of the Hawaiian Islands.

Opposite: clockwise from top left: 'awa (*Piper methysticum*); a native yellow 'ōhi'a lehua flower (*Metrosideros polymorpha*); fragrant coffee blossoms (*Coffea arabica*); Hawai'i's state flower, *Hibiscus brackenridgii*; sugar cane (*Saccharum officinarum*); noni (*Morinda citrifolia*).
Right: Puakala, a native Hawaiian prickly poppy (*Argemone glauca*).

Hawai'i Volcanoes National Park

On the Big Island of Hawai'i, a landscape that took more than seventy million years to create now welcomes more than 2.5 million visitors every year. This is Hawai'i Volcanoes National Park, one of the most active geological sites on earth.

Located on the southeastern edge of the island, the 230,000-acre park stretches from sea level to more than 13,000 feet at the summit of the earth's most massive volcano, Mauna Loa. One of two active volcanoes in the park, Mauna Loa dwarfs Kīlauea, the park's star attraction. Kīlauea means "spreading, much spewing," and lava has been flowing from this volcano for more than two decades, enlarging the island as it enters the Pacific.

As the lava cools, a new ecosystem emerges, and it is here that visitors will see firsthand how the Hawaiian Islands may have looked when they first rose from the sea. Small cracks in the crusty lava begin to trap airborne seeds, and new plants emerge from the barren landscape. Tufts of grasses, lichens, and small ferns cling for life in this desolate place

Left: Native ferns abound at Hawai'i Volcanoes National Park. The high altitude and misty weather create an ideal climate for tropical cloudforest plants.

and, as they decompose, soil forms to support new life. New plant life is nourished by deluges of rainfall, as much as twelve feet in a single year.

Eventually shrubs and trees emerge and create microclimates that host a wide variety of plant life. From the edges of recent lava flows to inland areas with dense native rainforests, Hawai'i Volcanoes National Park gives visitors a glimpse at this evolution in the landscape.

The diversity of plant life is impressive in the park. Here you will see native plants in their unmanicured state. Within the park live twenty-two species of endangered vascular plants. Terrestrial orchids and 'ōhia lehua flowers add a touch of color in a sea of green created by a wide variety of ferns. Koa trees (*Acacia koa*), with their sickle-shaped leaves, mingle with hāpu'u, Hawai'i's native tree ferns. The Thurston lava tube, a cave-like structure created by cooling lava, offers one of the best places to see a dense stand of native hapu'u. A cacophony of birds

Opposite: clockwise from top left: Native koa (*Acacia koa*) grow throughout the park; *Dodonaea viscosa*; a small orange lily grows with uluhe fern (*Dicranopteris* species); ground orchids (*Arundina bambusaefolia*) have naturalized in the park; an emerging fern fiddle; kāhili ginger (*Hedychium gardnerianum*).
Right: A path leads through the dense fern forests of the park to the lodge.

greets you as you descend rock-hewn walkways into a valley overwhelmed with foliage. Non-native kāhili ginger (*Hedychium gardnerianum*), with their intensely fragrant yellow trusses, remind you this is Hawai'i. Because these plants are aliens to the area, park officials have taken measures to eradicate them to improve the growth of the park's important endemic plants.

The United Nations named the park an international biosphere reserve and a world heritage site. Encompassing 150 miles of trails and 33,000 acres, the park's rainforest is the largest federal reserve in the United States.

With spectacular landscapes that come alive with the sounds of birds, the scent of ginger, and a broad range of rare and endangered plant life, Hawai'i Volcanoes National Park offers a glimpse of Hawai'i's beginning and its future as new land literally forms in front of your eyes.

Opposite: The scarlet red blossoms of the native ʻōhiʻa lehua (*Metrosideros polymorpha*) brighten the greenery of the park.
Above: Steam rises out of the Kīlauea Caldera, a lake of hardened lava.

Hawai'i Tropical Botanical Garden

Just outside of Hilo on the Big Island of Hawai'i, the old Māmalahoa Highway winds through dense jungles of century-old mango and breadfruit trees. Lush tropical foliage scented with the subtle essence of ginger envelops you as you travel the narrow road hugging Onomea Bay. This is the Hawai'i of your dreams.

Three decades ago, this paradise became the inspiration for one of Hawai'i's most diverse gardens. Vacationing with his wife Pauline, Dan Lutkenhouse purchased a seventeen-acre swatch of overgrown valley and began to create a public paradise. With pickaxe and shovel, Dan and his assistants cleared paths through the jungles, careful to preserve the natural beauty of the area. Using only hand labor, the work continued seven days a week for the next eight years until the garden opened to the public.

Left: Garden paths meander through dense vegetation, ending at the rugged ocean coastline.

Today, the garden is described by many as the most beautiful accessible tropical jungle garden in the world, attracting botanists, gardeners, and photographers from around the globe. The garden boasts a tropical collection of more than 2,000 species representing about 750 genera of plants.

Among the collections, the gingers, heliconias, and orchids stand out with their massive displays of exotic color. A state-of-the-art birdhouse with raucous macaws adds to the tropical experience.

The plants and animals enhance the natural beauty of the site, which includes a multi-tiered waterfall cascading through a palm jungle. And after you pass through the dense thicket of exotic plants, the view of Onomea Bay emerges, its waves crashing at your feet.

Dan and Pauline Lutkenhouse's determination testifies to the impact man can have on his environment. More than a million visitors (and counting) will forever have memories of the tropical splendor created by this family.

Left: A three-tiered waterfall cascades down the garden's steep terrain.
Opposite: clockwise from top left: *Alocasia micholitziana*; *Tapeinochilos ananassae*; *Aglaonema pictum*; pink banana (*Musa velutina*); *Heliconia indica var. striata*; *Heliconia bihai*.

Opposite: clockwise from far left: The garden's steep terrain is made accessible by carefully planned paths; *Heliconia orthotricha*; jackfruit (*Artocarpus heterophyllus*) bears the largest tree-borne fruit in the world, some weighing up to eighty pounds.
Above: Aglaonemas and marantas thrive in the shady garden. Gazebos provide shelter from the frequent rainshowers the garden receives.

Lili'uokalani Park and Gardens

When tsunamis hit the Big Island of Hawai'i in 1946 and 1960, the town of Hilo was destroyed by the killer waves. Entire city blocks were scoured clean of any trace of civilization. Buildings were tossed off their foundations and train tracks twisted like pretzels. But when you visit Hilo today, you are greeted by a peaceful historic town landscaped with towering banyan trees and emerald-green parks.

Among the town's most beautiful areas is the Waiākea Peninsula along Hilo Bay. Magnificent banyan trees, planted by visitors like Amelia Earhart, Richard Nixon, and Babe Ruth, arch over Banyan Drive as it hugs the bay. And nestled on thirty acres along the water, a Japanese garden entices visitors to stop and relax.

With its Edo-style gardens, pagodas, and stone lanterns, this is a typically Japanese garden. But look closer and you will see remnants of lava flows and tide pools; this could only be Hawai'i.

Left: Devastated by tsunamis, the Edo-style gardens and pagodas of Lili'uokalani Park and Gardens on Hilo Bay have been restored into one of Hawai'i's most beautiful Japanese gardens.

Above: Pagodas and Japanese-style structures give visitors a place to escape from the heat and sun.
Opposite: The park displays an impressive collection of Japanese statuary.

Lili'uokalani Park and Gardens was bequeathed by Queen Lili'uokalani, Hawai'i's last monarch, for public use. In the early 1900s, the land was fashioned into the largest Edo-style garden outside Japan as a memorial to Japanese immigrants who worked in the Waiākea sugar plantation. And although it has been destroyed by tsunamis twice since its creation, the garden is more beautiful than ever. In 1968, Japan presented the city with stone lanterns and wooden structures to commemorate the 100th anniversary of the arrival of Japanese immigrants. Curved bridges were replaced and the garden restored to its original splendor.

Today, you will find Fu dogs guarding the entrance to the park overlooking Hilo Bay and the Hāmākua Coast. The park has an open feel which allows you to survey the entire garden from the entrance. Bamboos, azaleas, and sago palms, native to Japan, are planted sparingly throughout the garden. Local Hawaiian plant life mingles with the traditional through the garden. Palms, bananas, hibiscus, and gingers complement the scenery, and ducks and ocean birds from the bay frequent the garden.

As you walk through the park, curving paths wind over lava formations, wood-

en bridges span small streams, and gazebos and benches invite you to relax as you enjoy the scenery. A traditional Japanese tea house is often used for tea ceremonies, and a canoe shelter houses Okinawan-style canoes that are used on Okinawan race days.

Because the park faces east on Hilo Bay, morning is the best time to enjoy it. The garden comes alive as fisherman cast nets in the nearby bay and joggers come to exercise. On sunny mornings, Mauna Kea Volcano, just west of the garden, rises above Hilo to create the perfect backdrop to this most Hawaiian area.

Lili'uokalani Park and Gardens is a serene escape from the cares of today and a tribute to yesterday, a memorial and ever-present reminder of Hawai'i's past.

Left: The park is located on Banyan Drive, Hilo's "Walk of Fame." Banyans (*Ficus microcarpa 'retusa'*) have been planted since the 1930s by the famous, including Cecil B. DeMille, Amelia Earhart, Louis Armstrong, Richard Nixon, and Babe Ruth.
Opposite: from left: Steps carved out of lava rock lead to an ocean view terrace; a Japanese-style lantern in front of a stand of striped bamboo (*Bambusa vulgaris vittata*); native loulu palms (*Pritchardia* species) blend with colorful crotons (*Codiaeum* hybrids).

Nani Mau Gardens

Twenty five years after opening its gates to the public, Nani Mau remains "forever beautiful" as its name implies. Located south of Hilo on the Big Island of Hawai'i, Nani Mau showcases a wide variety of exotic tropical plants on its fifty-three-acre site.

Founded by Makato Nitahara, the garden design is distinctly Japanese with manicured lawns and tightly cropped hedging. A Japanese-style bell tower stands like a sentinel over the heart of the garden. Built with twenty thousand individual timbers, the tower is jointed together like fine furniture without the need for nails or screws.

But the garden's plants are the star attractions here. Visitors can explore several theme gardens, including ginger, fruit tree, and hibiscus gardens. Palms, including brightly colored sealing wax palms (*Cyrtostachys renda*) complement the landscape. Visitors to the garden will discover several exotic finds, including a wide variety of rare tropical plants, such as a magnificent *Amherstia nobilis* tree.

Left: Manicured lawns add a sea of green to the brightly colored tropical plants at Nani Mau Gardens.

With more than 2,300 plants, Nani Mau houses one of the largest orchid collections in a public garden.

The garden provides several amenities, including a restaurant, gift shop, and shuttle service, making the site a perfect diversion for visitors to Hilo.

Left: A Japanese bell tower overlooks a bed of red gingers (*Alpinia purpurata*).
Opposite: clockwise from top left: The exotic flowering tree, *Amherstia nobilis*; the pagoda flower (*Clerodendrum paniculatum*); *Medinilla magnifica*; anthuriums; purple crinum (*Crinum procerum*);
Clinostigma ...

Opposite: clockwise from far left: A yellow flowering African tulip tree (*Spathodea campan-ulata*) shades a footpath; traveller's trees (*Ravenala madagascariensis*); Moses-in-the-cradle (*Rhoeo spathacea*) grows in the crevices of a lava rock wall.
Above: A Japanese lantern frames a view of the expansive lawn.

World Botanical Gardens

Just north of Hilo on the Big Island of Hawai'i, the picturesque Hāmākua Coast offers breathtaking views of the Pacific Ocean. If you are looking for a place to see the vestiges of Hawai'i's plantation days, this is the place. For more than a century, the Hāmākua Coast was the sugar cane capital of Hawai'i, but that all changed in the 1990s. As labor costs rose and sugar prices fell, the sugar mills closed their doors forever.

Today, as you drive the two-lane highway through the region, you pass smokestacks of abandoned mills and vast fields that remain fallow. Small plantation towns are relatively unchanged, but the streets are much quieter now.

In the small town of Umauma, sixteen miles north of Hilo, former sugar fields have been transformed into a 275-acre botanical garden. World Botanical Gardens, which opened to the public in 1995, now displays more than five thousand species of plants. Next to the visitors' center, the Rainbow Walk features one hundred species of bromeliads intermingling with orchids, crotons, and gingers.

Left: Spectacular three-tiered Umauma Falls is the star of the garden. African tulip trees (*Spathodea campanulata*), alexandra palms (*Archontophoenix alexandrae*) and kukui (*Aleurites moluccana*) blend with native trees.

With trees draped in vines, a canopied rainforest walk follows the path of a small stream, and a maze of mock orange invites visitors to lose themselves under the rustling fronds of Cuban royal palms (*Roystonea regia*). Scattered throughout the gardens, bananas, pineapples, papaya, and exotic fruit trees bear fruit in the ideal microclimate of the garden. Colorful shower trees (*Cassia* species) and rose apples (*Syzygium malaccense*) complement balsa wood, mahogany, and teak trees.

As you ascend the garden, the star attraction awaits you. Nestled in a valley carpeted with kukui nut (*Aleurites moluccana*) and tulip trees (*Spathodea campanulata*), with their bright orange flowers, Umauma Falls steps down the slope in a three hundred-foot tall three-tiered cascade.

With a 360-degree view from the slopes of Mauna Kea Volcano to the deep blue waters of the Pacific, World Botanical Garden provides visitors with a peaceful stop on a circle tour of Hawai'i's Big Island.

Left: Cook pines (*Araucaria columnaris*) stand like sentinels overlooking the Hāmākua Coast. **Opposite:** clockwise from top left: Mountain apple blossom (*Syzygium malaccense*); breadfruit (*Artocarpus altilis*); bromeliads and orchids; *Aechmea* bromeliads; multi-colored ti (*Cordyline fruticosa*); variegated hala, also called screwpine (*Pandanus baptistii*).

Gardens of Maui

Enchanting Floral Gardens of Kula Maui

When you enter the garden, the smell of white angel's trumpet (*Brugsmania* species) welcomes you to this beautiful eight-acre site. Clusters of exotic red and iridescent green jade vines dangle on arbors as you wander up the garden path.

The garden displays 1,500 species of plants from around the world, including protea, orchids, hibiscus, and fruit trees. Plumerias compel you to slow down and smell their intoxicating fragrance.

Bromeliads and other succulents, from agaves to euphorbias, thrive in this garden on the slopes of Haleakalā. Because of its elevation, Kula's climate allows Hawaiians to grow cool-climate plants that would suffer near the coast.

The garden includes a collection of Hawaiian native plants, including sandalwood (*Santalum ellipticum*) and yellow and red varieties of ʻōhiʻa lehua (*Metrosideros polymorpha*).

Left: Enchanting Floral Gardens of Kula Maui features an interesting collection of unusual plants, including jade vines and colorful bromeliads.

Vireyas, also called tropical rhododendrons, thrive in the cool climate and volcanic soil, similar to their native habitat in Malaysia.

At 2,500 feet above sea level, the garden's elevation provides cool weather year round, making it a good destination for visitors seeking an escape from the warmer weather of Maui's coastal areas.

Left: Red passion flower vine (*Passiflora coccinea*).
Opposite: clockwise from top left: leaf bases of the traveller's tree (*Ravenala madagascariensis*): hibiscus hybrid; Gloriosa lily *(Gloriosa superba)*; croton (*Codiaeum* hybrid); bromeliad flower spike (*Aechmea species*); pink *neoregelia* hybrid.

Opposite: from far left: Rocket pincushion protea (*Leucospermum reflexum*); purple orchid (*Vanda* hybrid); flaming sword bromeliad (*Vriesea splendens*).
Above, from left: An exotic flowering red jade vine *(Mucuna bennettii)*; a fragrant plumeria hybrid.

Kahanu Gardens

On Maui's northeastern coast, the picturesque village of Hāna greets visitors from all over the world who seek to experience the Hawai'i of yesterday. With its pristine waters and jungle-like rainforests, Hāna is a world apart from the bustle of Maui's golf-course resorts. Isolated from civilization by a narrow, winding road that hugs a craggy coastline, the town is home to a small village of residents, some of whom descend directly from Hawaiian royalty, or *ali'i*. Many who visit call Hāna Hawai'i's most "Hawaiian" place.

Just outside town, the remains of Hawai'i's largest ancient temple were rediscovered in the 1970s. The temple, or *heiau*, had been consumed by the jungles and lay hidden, perhaps for centuries. Covering more than three acres, the structure has been attributed to Chief Pi'ilani, Maui's ruler in the latter part of the sixteenth century, but carbon dating places construction at about A.D. 1294. Standing more than forty feet tall, the massive stone structure is now the centerpiece of one of Hawai'i's botanical treasures, Kahanu Gardens.

Left: Coconut palms (*Cocos nucifera*) grow on top of a forty-foot-tall Hawaiian temple built more than five hundred years ago. A native loulu palm (*Pritchardia arecina*) and ti plants (*Cordyline fruticosa*) flank the site.

Above: A plantation cottage houses crafts made from plants in the garden.
Opposite: With more than 120 different varieties, the garden maintains the largest bread-fruit (*Artocarpus altilis*) collection in the world.

In 1974, the Hāna Ranch and descendants of Chief Kahanu donated land to the former Pacific Tropical Botanical Garden (now called the National Tropical Botanical Garden) to create a botanical site. Subsequent donations and new purchases expanded the garden to its present size of nearly three hundred acres.

The garden now features a native Hawaiian plant collection as well as a sizeable garden displaying early Polynesian introductions. More than half the garden is blanketed by native screwpine, or hala (*Pandanus tectorius*), used by early Hawaiians for housing, mats, baskets, and canoe sails. The garden's hala forest is the largest in the Hawaiian Islands. The site is also home to one of Hawai'i's native palms, *Pritchardia affinis*, used by early Hawaiians to thatch their roofs.

A Canoe Garden includes important ethnobotanical plants that were brought to Hawai'i in canoes centuries ago. Taro, (*Colocasia esculenta*), sweet potato (*Ipomoea batatas*), sugar cane (*Saccharum officinarum*), kava (*Piper methysticum*), bananas (*Musa* species), and coconuts (*Cocos nucifera*) all played vital roles in early Hawaiian civilization.

The garden's breadfruit collection is especially noteworthy. With more than

120 varieties from eighteen Pacific Island groups, Indonesia, the Philippines, and the Seychelles, the garden displays the largest and most extensive collection of breadfruit varieties and species in the world.

With an historic national landmark as its focal point, this garden by the sea is a pleasure for history lovers as well as gardeners. The half-mile path that traverses the garden provides a peaceful walk in the park for visitors who wish to step back in time to the days of Hawaiian royalty.

Opposite: Sugar cane (*Saccharum officinarum*).
Above: Native hala, or screwpine (*Pandanus tectorius*) blankets nearly half the garden.

Kula Botanical Garden

On the slopes of Haleakalā, the district of Kula attracts visitors and locals to its cool, moist climate. This is up-country, an area where agriculture shares the spotlight with cattle ranching, far from the bustling beaches and resorts of West Maui.

As the tradewinds pass over Haleakalā, a vortex of wind brings a ring of clouds to the area every afternoon, clearing in time for perfect sunsets.

Kula is best known for its famous Maui onions, but the region is also home to flower growers and botanical gardens. Flowers that wither on the tropical coasts flourish in this cool but frost-free elevation.

When Warren McCord visited the area forty years ago, he stumbled upon a small verdant valley in the middle of a cattle ranch. With large rock outcroppings and waterfalls, the ravine seemed the perfect site for a botanical garden. McCord convinced the ranch owner to sell him seventeen acres, of which eight were established as a botanical garden.

Left: On the slopes of Haleakalā, Kula Botanical Garden offers a rich tapestry of plants that grow in cooler tropical climates.

Above: Blue hydrangeas (*Hydrangea macrophylla*) line a path to a gazebo which overlooks a gulch.
Opposite: clockwise from top left: A silver tree (*Leucadendron argenteum*); a spooned version of the Cape daisy (*Osteospermum 'Whirligig'*); orange canna flower; multi-colored bromeliad (*Neoreglia hybrid*); yellow *Banksia* flower; variegated leaf of *Canna* 'Tropicana.'

Today, the garden is home to more than 2,500 species that thrive at the garden's elevation of 2,300 feet. Pathways wind through garden beds planted with protea, orchids, and native plants, past waterfalls and koi ponds. Gazebos overlook the West Maui Mountains and the harbors of Māʻalaea and Kahului, making the site a perfect spot for a wedding.

Kula Botanical Garden also features exotic birds, including African cranes and endangered native nēnē geese, animating the peacefulness of this oasis on the slopes of a volcano.

Opposite: Protea cultivars, like 'Silver Mink,' abound in the garden.
Above: Cycads, ferns, and bromeliads border a garden path.

Gardens of Oʻahu

Dole Plantation

On the plains of central Oʻahu overlooking the North Shore, the Dole Plantation welcomes you to step back in time to the late nineteenth century when plantation life dominated the Hawaiian Islands. Through a collection of eight gardens, the history of life on the plantation and the plants and agricultural techniques of the 1800s are brought to life once more.

The site features a hibiscus garden, a lei garden, and a native species collection. Paths lined with mass plantings of bromeliads lead to waterfalls and grassy vistas. Dole, of course, is famous for its cultivation of the world's most popular bromeliad, the pineapple, and tour guides show visitors how to plant them in the garden.

Dole Plantation is also home to the world's largest maze. Shaped in the form of a pineapple, the maze covers more than two acres of pink hibiscus-lined paths. Crotons, heliconias, and pineapples are planted throughout the maze. Designed by the renowned Hawaiian landscape architec-

Left: With Hawaiʻi's Waiʻanae Mountains as a backdrop, Dole Plantation maintains an extensive collection of bromeliads, including a wide variety of pineapple species and cultivated specimens.

tural firm, Belt Collins, the maze has been listed by National Geographic's *Adventure Magazine* as one of America's Top 100 Adventures.

Dole Plantation pays tribute to founder James Dole on its Pineapple Express, a two-mile mini-train tour through an agricultural section of the garden, which includes a narration on the history of the pineapple industry in Hawai'i. Tropical trees such as lychee, banana, mango, papaya, cacao, and coffee grow along the route through the garden.

The Dole Plantation features a large visitors' center with a restaurant and gift shop, where customers learn how to prepare pineapple for the table. The site greets more than a million visitors each year and is a popular attraction for tourists circling the island on the way to the beaches of O'ahu's famous North Shore.

Opposite: clockwise from far left: Dole Plantation is home to the world's largest maze; Dole is best known for pineapples, and the garden displays varieties from around the world; plumeria hybrids perfume the air of the garden.
Right: A manmade waterfall and pond form the centerpiece of the garden.

Foster Botanical Garden

In 1853 Queen Kalama leased a small parcel of land to Dr. William Hillebrand, a German expatriate, to build a house and plant a garden. From these humble beginnings, Foster Botanical Garden was destined to become the first botanical garden in the Hawaiian Islands.

Hillebrand gained fame in Hawai'i for his work as a physician, international labor scout, and self-taught botanist. During his years in Hawai'i, Hillebrand catalogued Hawai'i's native plants in his life work, *Flora of the Hawaiian Islands*; and imported species from around the world, including the now-ubiquitous plumeria. Before he left the Islands, Hillebrand planted his garden with exotic trees that still grow at Foster.

After twenty-one years, William Hillebrand returned to Germany and his property was later sold to Captain Thomas and Mary Foster. Mary continued to plant new species, including the now-famous bo tree (*Ficus religiosa*) that

Left: A massive bo tree (*Ficus religiosa*) greets visitors to Foster Botanical Garden in Honolulu. The tree was planted by Mary Foster in 1913 and is a direct descendant of the tree in Gaya, India, under which, as the meditating Prince Gautama, Buddha received enlightenment.

greets visitors as they circle the garden. The bo tree is a clonal descendant of the tree Buddha sat under about 2,500 years ago.

Mary Foster solicited the help of Dr. Harold Lyon, a young botanist, to improve the garden. Upon her death in 1930, Mary bequeathed the property to the City of Honolulu to become the first public garden in Hawai'i. The garden officially opened its doors in 1931 as Foster Park.

As the garden's first director, Dr. Lyon enhanced the essential design of the garden and added an orchid collection. In his role as a researcher for the Hawai'i Sugar Planters' Association, Lyon introduced thousands of plants and trees to Hawai'i, a number of which he planted at Foster.

When Dr. Lyon died in 1957, he was succeeded by California landscape architect Paul Weissich. Under his direction, Foster Garden expanded to double its original size.

Today, the garden includes several theme areas, including the Upper Terrace, home to many of the original Hillebrand plantings, terraces with palms, aroids, gingers, and heliconias; a Prehistoric Glen; and the Lyon Orchid Garden. The Eco-

Opposite: A baobab tree (*Adansonia digitata*) is large enough to house a family. Native to Central Africa, the baobab trees supply, gum, rope fiber, paper, and cloth.
Above: A colorful display of bromeliads adds a splash of color near the garden's entrance.

Above: clockwise from top left: The garden features two kapok trees (*Ceiba pentandra*), easily identified by their massive foot-like roots; paved paths make the garden easy to access; the original Foster mansion once sat in the main terrace. All that remains is a vintage lampost; a whimsical sign directs visitors to various attractions.

Opposite: Native to Guiana, the cannonball tree (*Couroupita guianensis*) bears unusual fruit on its trunk.

nomic Garden displays a variety of useful plants that grow in the tropics, including cinnamon, cacao, breadfruit, allspice, and macadamia nut trees. With plantings dating back more than 150 years, the garden is a living museum of rare and exotic species from around the tropical world. The garden houses twenty-four of Oʻahu's "Exceptional Trees" that are protected by law.

The garden now greets more than forty-five thousand visitors every year who come to enjoy the splendor of Hawaiʻi's first botanical garden.

In addition to Foster as its flagship garden, the Honolulu Botanical Garden system now includes gardens throughout Oʻahu. Wahiawā, Koko Crater, Hoʻomaluhia and Liliʻuokalani Botanical Gardens give visitors to the island a sampling of the diverse climatic conditions around the island and the botanical jewels that flourish in tropical regions.

Above: Orchids and variegated pineapple plants (*Ananas comosus*) surround a gazebo.
Opposite: clockwise from top left: The fruit of the ivory cane palm (*Pinanga kuhlii*); a
striped bamboo (*Bambusa vulgaris vittata*); panama hat plant (*Carludovica palmata*); bananas grow in the Economic Garden; pink vanda orchids; vibrant orange bromeliads.

Opposite: clockwise from far left: A statue of Buddha; colorful leaves of a croton (*Codiaeum variegatum*); the palm leaf of a loulu (*Pritchardia* species) palm.
Above: Cycads and ferns line a shady walk through the garden.

Ho'omaluhia Botanical Garden

Rising more than three thousand feet, the dramatic peaks of the Ko'olau Mountains define the Windward Coast on the northeastern side of O'ahu. The remains of an ancient volcano, these jagged green mountains provide the perfect backdrop for one of Hawai'i's most enchanting gardens. This is the home of Ho'omaluhia Botanical Garden, the 400-acre jewel in the Honolulu Botanical Garden system.

Originally designed and built in conjunction with the U.S. Army Corps of Engineers to provide flood protection for the town of Kāne'ohe, the garden provides a serene respite for visitors looking to escape from the stresses of our modern world. Ho'omaluhia means "to make a place of peace and tranquility" in Hawaiian, fitting for this beautiful place. As you drive up the long, palm-lined drive, you are struck by the serenity of the place. Your blood pressure drops as the noise of civilization is replaced by the soothing sounds of songbirds singing in the rainforest. The scent of the tropics and the grandeur of the surroundings affirm you have entered a special place.

Left: The Ko'olau Mountain Range, vestiges of an extinct volcano, provide a dramatic backdrop to this grouping of hala, also called screwpine (*Pandanus tectorius*).

Ho'omaluhia's theme gardens include impressive plantings of Hawaiian natives, as well as plants from Polynesia, Africa, tropical America, Southeast Asia, Melanesia, Sri Lanka, India, and the Philippines. Paul Weissich, then director of the Honolulu Botanical Gardens, spent years collecting and planting rare seeds from around the tropical world. Those seeds have matured into the lush, exotic landscape visitors see today.

The garden's thirty-two-acre lake provides the perfect spot to enjoy an afternoon picnic or a view of the breathtaking Ko'olau Mountains, and bikers can spend a leisurely afternoon exploring the gardens on fifteen miles of trails.

The garden's paths take you on a journey past stands of colorful heliconias, tropical flowering trees, and exotic palms. Every season brings a new experience here. In December, the sweet smell of nutmeg blossoms perfume the air; in March, the scent of plumerias signal the arrival of spring. And throughout the year, the ever-changing weather of O'ahu's Windward Coast sets the mood in the garden. In an instant, blue skies are replaced by a sudden rainshower and dozens of short-lived waterfalls, reminding you that you are in the tropics.

Opposite: Colorful Hawaiian ti hybrids (*Cordyline fruticosa*) surround the visitors' center.
Above: clockwise from left: Paved roads make it easy to explore Hoʻomaluhia's four hundred-acre grounds; a banyan tree provides a shady resting place; palms cascade down the hillside of a natural amphitheater.

Above: Mexican fan palms (*Washingtonia robusta*) tower over the thirty-two-acre lake at Ho'omaluhia.
Opposite: clockwise from left: waterfowl gather at the lake; a native white hibiscus (*Hibiscus arnottianus*); a native red *Hibiscus clayi.*

In addition to the extensive tropical plant collections, the garden houses a visitors' center, an art gallery, and picnic pavilions. On the weekends, visitors can fish in the lake or camp overnight at one of several campsites. Bird lovers will enjoy the two endangered water fowl that make the lake their home, the Hawaiian coot ('Ala eke'oke'o) and the Hawaiian gallinule ('Alae'ula). Ho'omaluhia even features wedding sites throughout the garden.

Although you can drive through the garden on paved roads, Ho'omaluhia takes more than a day to fully appreciate. You will return to this garden again and again. This is paradise; one of the secret treasures on the Island of O'ahu.

Left: Native plants, like this koa (*Acacia koa*), grow throughout the garden.
Opposite: clockwise from top left: New palm leaves emerge in shades of salmon on *Ptychosperma waitianum*; the stilt-like roots of hala, or screwpine (*Pandanus tectorius*); nutmeg fruit (*Myristica fragrans*); ti hybrid (*Cordyline fruticosa*); the warty fruit of the Leichhardt tree (*Nauclea orientalis*); the red pods of the lipstick plant (*Bixa orellana*).

Opposite: clockwise from left: Vivid red sealing wax palms (*Cyrtostachys renda*) line a path near the visitors' center; the orange collar palm (*Areca vestiaria*) bears a bright orange crownshaft and colorful fruit; orange flowers of a *Brownea* tree.

Above: With their bright orange or yellow flowers, African tulip trees (*Spathodea campanulata*) provide a splash of color in the dense green of the garden. Although non-native and highly invasive, the trees are nonetheless beautiful.

Kapiʻolani Park

At the east end of Waikīkī, Kapiʻolani Regional Park has greeted visitors since 1876. Named for King Kalākaua's wife, Queen Kapiʻolani, the site was later conveyed to the Republic of Hawaiʻi to remain in perpetuity as a free park, hosting a wide variety of outdoor activities.

Perhaps best known as the home of the Honolulu Zoo and the Waikīkī Shell, the park's towering trees and dramatic views of Diamond Head attract visitors looking for a shady picnic site away from the noise of neighboring Waikīkī.

Including Diamond Head, the park encompasses five hundred acres with trees that date back more than one hundred years. In its center, a small botanical garden features colorful poincianas, bouganvilleas and native Hawaiian plants, including *Pritchardia* palms and native hibiscus.

For visitors to Honolulu looking for an easy place to experience Hawaiʻi's botanical past, Kapiʻolani Regional Park is just steps from the hotels of Waikīkī.

Left: A bright golden royal poinciana (*Delonix regia f. flavida*) greets visitors to the small botanical garden in the center of Kapiʻolani Regional Park. The garden is an easy walk from Waikīkī.

Opposite: from far left: A dwarf poinciana (*Caesalpinia pulcherrima*); a native red *Hibiscus clayi*; the purple bracts of a bougainvillea.
Above: The garden offers a close-up view of O'ahu's landmark, Diamond Head.

Koko Crater Botanical Garden

On the southeast corner of the Island of O'ahu, the remainders of Hawai'i's volcanic past rise above the villages and beaches of the island. Massive tuff cones, formed when volcanic ash erupted from vents during eruptions from Ko'olau Volcano, punctuate the landscape. The most recognized in the series is Diamond Head, which rises more than seven hundred feet over Waikīkī, the most famous beach in the world.

But as you pass the bend toward the Windward Coast, a larger tuff cone dominates the landscape. This is Koko Crater, now home to a botanical garden for dryland tropical plants, a perfect location since this side of the island receives a negligible amount of rainfall. Rising more than 1,200 feet above sea level, Koko Crater is the tallest tuff cone on O'ahu. Inside its massive walls, the crater has been transformed into a botanical garden with more than sixty acres of plantings. Actually a complex of two craters, the site was reserved in 1958 and now, a half century later, the site is emerging as a concept garden featuring drought-tolerant plants.

Left: The outer crater of the Koko Crater complex houses a vast collection of hybrid plumerias and bougainvilleas.

The garden includes several significant plant collections. As you enter the crater, the scent of plumeria from the Dean Conklin Plumeria Grove perfumes the air. The grove is home to a seemingly endless forest of mature cultivars, ranging from white to red to multi-colored. These pinwheel flowers are Hawai'i's emblem, and no other botanical garden in the Islands contains such a large collection.

Many visitors end their tour here, but further down the dry path, colorful hybrid bougainvillea vines blanket the hillsides as you enter the heart of the crater. Here, you begin your journey on a two-mile loop through the inner basin. Naturalized kiawe and koa haole trees dominate the landscape. The garden is divided into four distinct areas representing various parts of the world. The Americas region features a display of cacti and other desert plantings.

The Hawaiian section is home to a grove of wiliwili trees (*Erythrina sandwicensis*), endemic to Hawai'i. This impres-

Opposite: clockwise from top left: A multi-colored plumeria hybrid; an octopus cactus (*Rathbunia alamosensis*); a desert rose (*Adenium obesum*); flowers of the native wiliwili (*Erythrina sandwicensis*); a cycad cone; the spiny trunk of a *Pachypodium geayi*.
Right: The garden includes a grove of native wiliwili trees (*Erythrina sandwicensis*).

Above: Cacti and succulents thrive in the dry, sunny climate inside Koko Crater.
Opposite: The garden features a collection of drought-tolerant palms, including Mexican fan palms (*Washingtonia robusta*), blue hesper palms (*Brahea armata*), and Mediterranean fan palms *(Chamaerops humilis).*

sive stand is now protected by Hawai'i state law.

Further down the path, plants from Madagasgar and Africa emerge from the dry crater floor. Sanseveria blanket the bases of trees and the flowers of a mass planting of desert rose (*Adenium obesum*) add a blaze of color. Massive baobab trees from Africa tower over cycads and aloes, and *Gardenia volkensii,* with its baseball-sized seed pods, provides a hint of fragrance from its small white flowers.

In the heart of the crater, a palm collection displays species from around the world that thrive in dry sunny areas. Blue hesper palms (*Brahea armata*) from Mexico harmonize with date palms from Africa and Bismarck palms (*Bismarckia nobilis*) from Madagascar.

Koko Crater Botanical Garden is a work-in progress for the Honolulu Botanical Gardens. As its plantings mature, the garden is becoming an important inspiration for gardeners in the dry tropics, and a conservation garden for rare and endangered dryland species.

Lili'uokalani Botanical Garden

Near the base of Punchbowl Crater, a reminder of Hawai'i's volcanic past, a small garden goes largely unnoticed by most who visit O'ahu. Located in the heart of bustling Honolulu, the garden offers a serene spot to enjoy a picnic lunch next to a small waterfall and a bubbling stream. This is Lili'uokalani Botanical Garden, the smallest treasure in the Honolulu Botanical Garden system.

Once owned by Queen Lili'uokalani, Hawai'i's last sovereign queen, the garden had once been a picnic spot for her too. One can imagine the former days of the Hawaiian monarchy when the queen walked through the garden, enjoying the same serenity we enjoy today.

Shortly after she gained power in 1891, the queen attempted to draft a new constitution that would restore the monarchy and return powers lost to the throne by the previous monarch, King Kalākaua. The queen was arrested on weapons charges by the provisional government on January 16, 1895, and sentenced to imprisonment in 'Iolani Palace, just blocks from the garden. After abdicat-

Left: Waikahalulu Falls provides a soothing escape in the middle of bustling Honolulu.

ing the throne, the queen lived at nearby Washington Place until her death in 1917 at age seventy-nine.

Lili'uokalani bequeathed the land to the City of Honolulu to be used for the public's enjoyment. Today, the seven-acre garden is developing into a special place where visitors will see native Hawaiian plants and tropical gingers. A cathedral of monkeypod trees (*Samanea saman*) shades the garden and stream, and picnic tables by the waterfall allow visitors to enjoy an open-air lunch.

A small footbridge traverses the rocky borders of Nu'uanu Stream, which intersects the garden. And on the other side, a grassy field entices you to roll out a blanket and sit under the shade of towering trees, enjoying the peaceful sound of water cascading over Waikahalulu Falls.

If you are looking for O'ahu's most accessible waterfall, you have found it. With Foster Botanical Garden just minutes away, Lili'uokalani Botanical Garden offers visitors a pleasant place to sit and enjoy the special gift left to you by Hawai'i's last monarch.

Opposite: clockwise from left: White ginger (*Hedychium coronarium*); blue ginger (*Dichorisandra thyrsiflora*); Hawaiian cotton blossom, also called mao (*Gossypium tomentosum*).
Right: Pink ginger (*Alpinia purpurata cv. Eileen MacDonald*) frame the view of Waikahalulu Falls.

Lyon Arboretum

In the hills of Mānoa above Honolulu, a tropical rainforest with exotic trees, brilliant heliconias, and fragrant gingers welcomes visitors to explore the Hawai'i of their fantasies. Narrow paths hewn out of volcanic soil ascend through lush acres of palms and fern forests, ending at a soothing waterfall. This is Lyon Arboretum, a 194-acre botanical garden with one of the most diverse plant collections on O'ahu.

Sitting under a bo tree (*Ficus religiosa*), you enjoy a garden that was established, not for leisure, but out of necessity. As you walk through the dense vegetation of the garden, it is hard to believe you are walking on land that was once a barren wasteland. By the early twentieth century, O'ahu faced a crisis that would threaten its emerging settlements. Early cattle farmers allowed their livestock to range free in the mountains above Honolulu, stripping bare the vital watershed that supplies most of the water to the island. Efforts by the Territorial Board of Agriculture and Forestry to restore the watershed with native trees had failed; the soil could no longer sustain their growth.

Left: A path and footbridge lead to the Hawaiian native and ethnobotanical collections.

Above: The visitors' center is surrounded by a lush tropical landscape that includes native and introduced species, like this *Alcantera imperialis* in the foreground.
Opposite: Palms are plentiful at Lyon Arboretum. The fruit of the Highland betel nut palm (*Areca ipot*) adds a bright accent to the dense vegetation of a garden trail.

And early introductions, including iron-wood trees and eucalyptus, did not retain the run-off.

In 1918, as World War I drew to a close, the Hawaiian Sugar Planters' Association created an experimental garden on the site to restore the watershed and grow economically significant plants. Called Haukulu, the land had once belonged to Charles Kana'ina, father of King William Lunalilo. The sugar planters hired a young botanist from Minnesota, Dr. Harold Lyon, to manage the project that became known as Mānoa Arboretum. The land provided a test site for reforestation as well as a trial plot for sugar cane, which was grown in the area until the 1940s.

Over the next forty years, Lyon introduced about two thousand tree and plant species to the site. Shortly before he died, Lyon convinced the Hawaiian Sugar Planters' Association to convey the arboretum to the University of Hawai'i, stipulating it be kept in perpetuity as an arboretum and botanical garden.

In the 1950s, the university shifted the focus from forestry to horticulture, and began planting ornamental and economically useful plants, more that two thousand species in all. Today, the garden

serves as a tropical Eden for visitors and a research station for botanists. The garden is nationally recognized for its propagation of rare and endangered Hawaiian plants and for its extensive collection of tropical ornamentals. At every turn, visitors are treated to the rare and unusual, from the exotic scarlet flowers of *Amherstia nobilis* to the wide selection of rare and unusual gingers, heliconias, and palms. Every season brings change to the garden when brilliant flowers emerge out of the endless sea of green.

To appreciate the full beauty of the garden, visitors should spend a full morning or an afternoon on the narrow footpaths winding through dense, jungle-like forests to the small but beautiful 'Aihualama Falls. In the center of the garden, a manicured lawn invites visitors to sit and enjoy a snack or picnic lunch, serenaded by the cacophony of sounds emanating from the rainforest. Mynahs, cardinals,

Left: A statue of a walking Buddha stands under a bo tree (*Ficus religiosa*).
Opposite: clockwise from top left: The bracts of *Heliconia bihai*; pink fruit of the *Medinilla cumingii*; a tropical vireya rhododendron hybrid; an ornamental pink-fruited banana (*Musa velutina*); a flowering T*hunbergia mysorensis* vine; the fuzzy bracts of *Heliconia vellerigera*.

wild parrots, and cockatoos have made the arboretum their permanent home, completing the experience of paradise in Hawai'i. For visitors looking for a quiet place away from the bustle of Waikīkī and Honolulu, this is it.

Opposite: clockwise from left: 'Aihualama Waterfall marks the end of the trail at Lyon Arboretum; the black bat flower (*Tacca chantrieri*); a hybrid anthurium.
Right: Harrison Drive cut through the dense growth at Lyon.

Above: A path meanders through a series of tropical plantings that include gingers, heliconias, palms, mondo grass, and a variegated ficus.
Opposite: clockwise from top left: Cobblestone paths lead through the manmade jungle; *Mussaenda 'Dona Luz'*; groupings of palms are common in the landscape.

Opposite: clockwise from left: A lotus flower emerges from a reflecting pool; the variegated leaves of *Sanchezia speciosa*; *Vriesea imperialis*.
Above: A gazebo provides shelter from the garden's frequent rain showers.

University of Hawai'i Japanese Garden

Nestled in the emerald green slopes of the Ko'olau Mountains, the University of Hawai'i at Mānoa is a botanical wonderland. Shower trees (*Cassia* species) line the campus roadways, and heliconias and plumerias border campus dwellings. As you explore further, you discover a garden that most visitors will never see. Behind the East-West Center, a Japanese garden invites visitors to enjoy its simplicity.

Created in 1963 by Japanese landscape architect Kenzo Ogata, the garden is considered one of America's finest. At its entrance, a traditional Japanese tea house is perched over a small waterfall that leads to a meandering stream. The leaves of bamboo and lady palms (*Raphis excelsa*) flutter in the tradewinds as you walk through the grassy lawn. Japanese lanterns watch over the koi that swim in the stream.

This garden provides a quick diversion to anyone visiting the campus, and an inspiration to gardeners planning a Japanese-themed garden.

Left: A manmade waterfall feeds a stream that divides the garden.

Above: A Japanese lantern overlooks a stream stocked with koi. Bonsai are scattered througout the park.

Above: clockwise from left: The lady palm (*Rhapis excelsa*) is native to Japan; variegated pothos vines (*Epipremnum aureum*) thrive in the shade of the garden's tall trees; the garden's small lawn is a frequent resting spot for visitors to the garden.

Wahiawā Botanical Garden

Between the Waiʻanae and Koʻolau Mountain Ranges on the Island of Oʻahu, a gently sloping plain stretches from Pearl Harbor to the North Shore. Here, at an elevation of about one thousand feet, planters have been growing crops for more than a century, among them Hawaiʻi's most famous: pineapples and sugar cane.

In the small village of Wahiawā, the Hawaiʻi Sugar Planters' Association established an experimental arboretum, similar to their larger site in Mānoa, in the 1920s. Under the direction of Dr. Harold Lyon, the site was planted with a variety of trees from around the tropic world, many of which still grace the garden. In 1957, the arboretum was converted to a botanical garden, now part of the Honolulu Botanical Garden system.

A tour through the twenty-seven-acre garden reveals a palette of plantings that thrive in cooler, wetter elevations in the tropics. The garden's canopy of mature trees creates the atmosphere of a tropical rainforest filled with shade-loving plants from around the world. Tall rainbow euca-

Left: Trees planted by the Hawaiʻi Sugar Planters' Association in the 1920s create a canopy for Wahiawā Botanical Garden in the center of the Island of Oʻahu.

lyptus trees (*Eucalyptus deglupta*), with their trunks striped in green, purple, and red, greet visitors as they enter the garden. The scent of nutmeg (*Myristica fragrans*) fills the air every winter, and blue gingers and heliconias provide seasonal color.

The garden is organized into several collections displaying native Hawaiian plants, as well as palms, aroids, ferns, heliconias, calatheas, and epiphytes. Native loulu palms (*Pritchardia species*) and hāpuʻu ferns (*Cibotium chamissoi*) complement heliconias from South America and bamboos from Asia. And the original planting of cinnamon, chicle, kauri, and earpod trees reflect the garden's history as an arboretum for useful trees. Visitors can follow the self-guided tour along the paved sidewalk on the upper terrace or descend into a ravine to enjoy the native Hawaiian plantings.

Located close to the famous Dole Plantation, Wahiawā Botanical Garden is a worthy diversion for visitors seeking a shady side trip in a cool rainforest.

Left: The bark of the rainbow eucalyptus (*Eucalyptus deglupta*) sheds to create a rainbow of colors from yellow to green to purple.
Opposite, left to right: Orange spiral ginger flower buds (*Costus* species) are sometimes used as a shampoo and conditioner; a lobster claw (*Heliconia rostrata*) brightens the garden's Heliconia Walk.

Above: The upper terrace of the garden allows visitors to wander around vine-covered trees, many of which were planted more than a half century ago. More adventurous visitors will descend into a densely vegetated gulch filled with Hawaiian natives.
Right: Brazilian red cloak (*Megaskepasma erythrochlamys*) flowers profusely in the dappled shade of the garden.

Waimea Valley

Long before the first contact by European settlers, Waimea Valley held an important spot in Hawai'i's culture. A center of religious significance, the valley holds clues to its storied past. Remnants of ancient stone temples, called heiaus, and agricultural sites dot the landscape, some dating back to the twelfth century. Throughout the valley, Hawaiians grew taro, sweet potato, bananas, and other crops, clearing the fertile valley for cultivation.

Centuries later, the valley would become home to an adventure park featuring cliff divers and horseback rides. In 2003, the National Audubon Society assumed management of the 1,900-acre valley, focusing on the botanical garden and conservation, restoring native flora and documenting the diversity of the valley.

Today, visitors will experience a nature walk that meanders through the valley for more than three miles, rising

Left: Waimea Valley's 1,900-acre site features a vast array of native and introduced tropical plants.

from sea level to more than one thousand feet. The site features thirty-six botanical collections, displaying more than five thousand species of tropical plants.

The valley includes one of the world's best Hawaiian ethnobotanical gardens with a significant collection of rare and endangered species. Terraces featuring plants from tropical Asia, Guam, Madagascar, the Seychelles Islands, Lord Howe Island, Sri Lanka, and the Bonin Islands add to the diversity of the garden.

The raucous calls of peacocks echo through the valley as you explore gardens dedicated to specific plant groups. The Hibiscus Evolutionary Garden displays exotic flowers from around the world, including rare Hawaiian natives. The Bauhinia Garden comes alive with its orchid-like flowers in all shades of mauve, purple, and scarlet. And the brilliant waxy flowers of the Heliconia Garden glow in the dappled shade of a canopy of monkeypod trees.

Throughout the garden, the sweet fragrance of lilies and gingers perfumes the

Opposite: clockwise from top left: *Hibiscus schizopetalus*; *Bauhinia galpinii*; a rainbow shower tree (*Cassia* cultivar); *Heliconia bihae*; *Heliconia mariae*; chenille plant (*Acalypha hispida*).
Right: Sunbeams brighten a stone pathway.

air, and the experience of the tropics is everywhere. Epyphitic ferns cling to tree branches, colorful bougainvillea and passionfruit vines drape the cliffsides, and bamboo forests beckon visitors to tap on their hollow stems.

At the end of the journey, Waimea Falls cascades down a volcanic slope to feed Kamananui Stream, which flows through the garden to the sea.

And, as a special treat, visitors can swim in a freshwater pool under the forty-foot waterfall, enveloped in the garden's dense vegetation and the serenade of exotic birds.

Located across from Waimea Bay, famous as one of the top surfing beaches in the world, the garden is easy to recommend to anyone seeking an easy nature hike into a pristine, tropical valley.

Opposite: Waimea Falls is a focal point of the garden.
Above: Paths wind throughout the canopied garden.

Resources

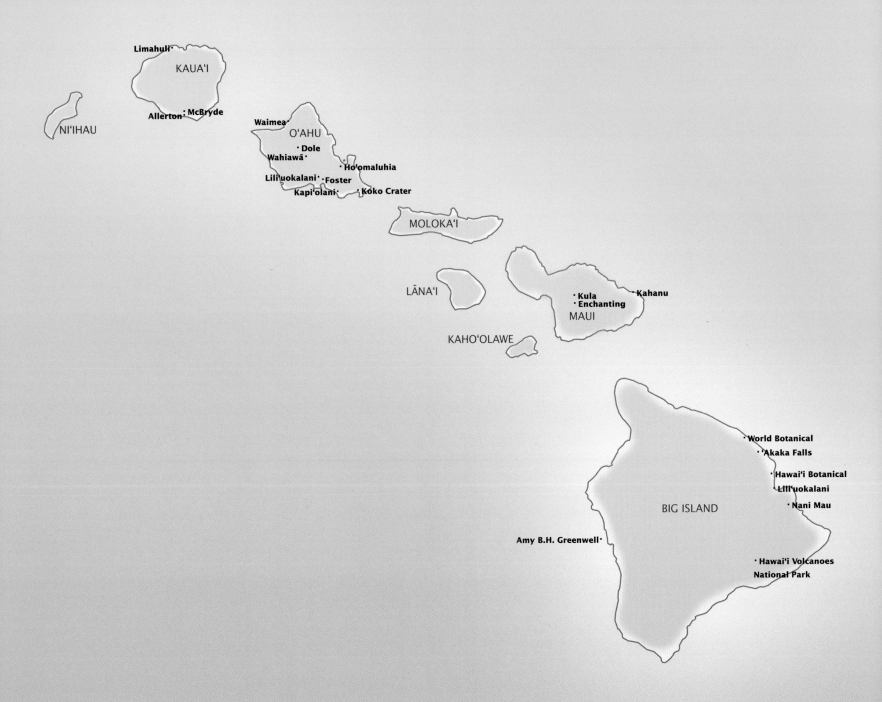

Limahuli ·

KAUA'I

Allerton · · **McBryde**

NI'IHAU

Waimea ·

O'AHU

· **Dole**

Wahiawā ·

· **Ho'omaluhia**

Lili'uokalani · · **Foster**

Kapi'olani · · **Koko Crater**

MOLOKA'I

LĀNA'I

· **Kula** · **Kahanu**

· **Enchanting**

MAUI

KAHO'OLAWE

· **World Botanical**

· **Akaka Falls**

· **Hawai'i Botanical**

· **Lili'uokalani**

· **Nani Mau**

BIG ISLAND

Amy B.H. Greenwell ·

· **Hawai'i Volcanoes**

National Park

Public Gardens

From lush rainforests to dryland gardens, the Hawaiian Islands feature gardens that display plants from nearly every climatic zone. The gardens featured in this book represent a sampling of the botanical wonders you will find throughout the Islands.

Kaua'i

Allerton Garden
4425 Lāwa'i Road
Kōloa, Hawai'i 96756
(808) 742-2623
http://ntbg.org/

On the southern coast of Kaua'i, Allerton Garden is one of two gardens in the Lāwa'i Valley. The garden includes formal outdoor living areas, statuary, and tropical fruit gardens. Queen Emma, wife of King Kamehameha IV, planted a variety of tropical plants, some of which survive in the garden. Tours are guided. Open daily. The visitor's center is across from Spouting Horn near Po'ipū Beach on Kaua'i's southern coast. Admission fee.

McBryde Garden
4425 Lāwa'i Road
Kōloa, Hawai'i 96756
(808) 742-2623
http://ntbg.org/

Formerly a sugar plantation, McBryde Garden is a lush 252-acre valley garden with extensive plantings of palms, native plants, and early Polynesian introductions. McBryde serves as a research and conservation garden and is adjacent to Allerton Garden. Open daily. Call for hours and admission fees.

Limahuli Garden and Preserve
Mailing address
P.O. Box 808
Hanalei, Hawai'i 96714
http://ntbg.org/
(808) 826-1053

Limahuli Garden is set in a tropical valley on the north shore of Kaua'i. Selected by the American Horticultural Society as the best natural botanical garden in the United States, Limahuli Garden displays ancient taro terraces built nearly a century ago. Features an extensive collection of native plants, including loulu (*Pritchardia*) palms. The entire garden includes a 17-acre public garden and 985 acres of preserve. Located in Hā'ena, one-half mile past the nine-mile marker on Kuhiō Highway #560. Call for information and admission fee.

Big Island

'Akaka Falls State Park
Highway 220
Hilo, Hawai'i

Located at the end of Highway 220, just eleven miles west of Hilo, the park's star attraction is its namesake waterfall, plunging more than four hundred feet to a pool below. Lush, jungle-like paths loop through the garden, requiring visitors to descend several steep staircases. An excellent location for an afternoon picnic. Open from dawn to dusk. No entrance fee.

Amy B.H. Greenwell
Enthnobotanical Garden
P.O. Box 1053
Captain Cook, Hawai'i 96704
(808) 323-3318
http://www.bishopmuseum.org/exhibits/greenwell/greenwell.html

Located on the Kona Coast in Captain Cook, the garden is located twelve miles south of Kailua-Kona at mile marker 110. The fifteen-acre garden focuses on Hawaiian plants, including endemic and introduced Polynesian species. Donations accepted.

Hawai'i Tropical Botanical Garden
27-717 Old Māmalahoa Highway
P.O. Box 80
Pāpa'ikou, Hawai'i 96781
808-964-5233
http://www.htbg.com

Located eight miles north of Hilo on the four-mile Scenic Route, this garden cascades down a slope to Onomea Bay. Stands of Alexandra palms have naturalized on the hillsides. The garden is carved out of a gulch that opens to the bay below. Open seven days a week from 9 A.M. to 4 P.M. Tours are self-guided and maps are provided. Admission fee.

Hawai'i Volcanoes National Park
P.O. Box 52
Hawai'i National Park, Hawai'i 96718
(808) 985-6000
http://www.nps.gov/havo/

Located thirty minutes southwest of Hilo on Highway 11, the park is a forty-five-minute drive from town center. Established in 1916, the park encompasses 333,000 acres, including the world's most massive and active volcanoes. An ideal location to see endemic plants and animals. Open 24 hours a day year round. Admission fee.

Lili'uokalani Park and Gardens
Banyan Drive
Hilo, Hawai'i 96720

This thirty-acre park on Hilo's Banyan Drive features a beautiful Japanese garden that overlooks Hilo Bay. Much of the park is landscaped in Edo-style gardens, with pergolas, lanterns, and statuary throughout the garden. No entrance fee.

Nani Mau Gardens
421 Makalika Street
Hilo, Hawai'i 96720
(808) 959-3500
http://www.nanimau.com/

This twenty-acre garden outside Hilo includes an orchid house, anthurium garden, and fine collection of colorful tropical plants, including the beautiful *Amherstia nobilis* tree. Open daily, including holidays, from 9 A.M. to 4 P.M. Admission fee.

World Botanical Gardens
16 Mile Marker, Highway 19
Honomū, Hawai'i 96728
(808) 963-5427
http://www.wbgi.com

Just north of Hilo, this garden displays more than five thousand plant species and Umauma Falls, a three-tiered three hundred foot waterfall. Open daily from 9 A.M to 5 P.M. Admission fee.

Maui

Enchanting Floral Gardens of Kula
Maui
Kula, Hawai'i
(808) 878-2531
http://www.flowersofmaui.com

Located on Kula Highway (Highway 37) at the 10 mile marker, this eight-acre garden includes a nice collection of bromeliads and protea, as well as exotic red and green jade vines. In all, the garden contains more than 1,500 species of tropical and subtropical plants. Open daily 9 A.M. to 5:00 P.M. Admission fee.

Kahanu Gardens
650 'Ula'ino Road
Hāna, Hawai'i
(808) 248-8912
http://ntbg.org/

Home to Pi'ilanihale Heiau, believed to be the largest ancient place of worship in Polynesia. Features native plants and early Polynesian introductions. Open weekdays from 10 A.M. to 2 P.M. Admission fee.

Kula Botanical Garden
Kula, Hawai'i
(808) 878-1715

Located on Kekaulike Highway (Highway 377) near the intersection of Kula Highway (Highway 37), the six-acre garden was established in 1977 as a native Hawaiian plant reserve. The garden's collection includes orchids, proteas, bromeliads, and native plants. Exotic African cranes, ponds with koi, and endangered Hawaiian nēnē geese also call the garden home. Open daily from 9 A.M. until 4 P.M. Admission fee.

O'ahu

Dole Plantation Gardens
64-1550 Kamehameha Highway
Wahiawā, Hawai'i 96786
Telephone: (808) 621-8408
http://www.dole-plantation.com/

About a forty-minute drive from Waikīkī on the way to the North Shore, the garden features eight separate displays, including a vast collection of bromeliads and hibiscus. The Pineapple Garden maze is the largest in the world, created from a 1.7 mile hibiscus hedge. Call for hours and admission fee.

Foster Botanical Garden
50 North Vineyard Boulevard
Honolulu, Hawai'i 96817
(808) 522-7065
http://www.co.honolulu.hi.us/parks/hbg/fbg.htm

Planted in the 1850s, Foster Botanical Garden is the oldest of the Honolulu Botanical Gardens. This fourteen-acre garden has an excellent collection of palms and exceptional trees. Open daily from 9 A.M. to 4 P.M. except holidays. Admission fee.

Ho'omaluhia Botanical Garden
45-680 Luluku Road
Kāne'ohe, Hawai'i 96744
(808) 233-7323
http://www.co.honolulu.hi.us/parks/hbg/hmbg.htm

Ho'omaluhia displays plantings from the major tropical regions with a special emphasis on native Hawaiian plants. More than four hundred acres of gardens with a jaw-dropping view of the Ko'olau Mountains. Open daily from 9 A.M. to 4 P.M., except some holidays. No entrance fee. Campgrounds with bathroom facilities are provided free of charge. Guided nature hikes are offered.

Kapi'olani Park
3902 Pākī Ave., P.O. Box 3059
Honolulu, Hawai'i 96815
http://www.kapiolanipark.org/

Located at the foot of Diamond Head off Kapahulu Avenue, the park is Hawai'i's oldest. The 500-acre site includes a small botanical garden with native palms, hibiscus, poincianas, and bougainvilleas. A ten-minute walk from the hotels on Waikīkī Beach. No entrance fee.

Koko Crater Botanical Garden
Kealahou Street, inside Koko Crater
(808) 522-7060
http://www.co.honolulu.hi.us/
parks/hbg/kcbg.htm

This sixty-acre garden is located inside Koko Crater on the eastern side of the island and displays a good selection of plants for dry gardens. No entrance fee.

Lili'uokalani Botanical Garden
114 North Kuakini Street
Honolulu, Hawai'i 96817

Just a few blocks from Foster Botanical Garden, this 7.5-acre garden is devoted to native Hawaiian plants, but the waterfall and canopy of trees make the site a perfect picnic stop. Open daily from 9 A.M. to 4 P.M. except for Christmas Day and New Year's Day. No entrance fee.

Lyon Arboretum
3860 Mānoa Road
Honolulu, Hawai'i 96822
(808) 988-0456
www.hawaii.edu/lyonarboretum

At the upper end of Mānoa Road, this 194-acre garden features an extensive collection of tropical plant-

ings in a lush rainforest setting. Close to Waikīkī and University of Hawai'i, the garden is open weekdays from 9 A.M. to 4 P.M., except holidays. Closed on weekends. Guided tours offered on some days. Call (808) 988-0456 for reservations. Donations accepted.

University of Hawai'i
Japanese Garden
1601 East West Road
Honolulu, Hawai'i 96848
Telephone: (808) 944-7111
http://www.botany.Hawai'i.edu/faculty/carr/160webindex.htm

Located in lower Mānoa Valley, the campus is planted throughout with impressive tropical plantings. Created in 1963 by Japanese landscape architect Kenzo Ogata, the Japanese garden is considered one of America's finest. Open daily from dawn to dusk. No entrance fee.

Wahiawā Botanical Garden
1396 California Avenue
Wahiawā, Hawai'i 96786
Phone: (808) 621-5463
http://www.co.honolulu.hi.us/
parks/hbg/wbg.htm

Developed by sugar planters in the 1920s the garden now encompasses twenty-weven acres of tropical rainforest gardens, including native plants, exceptional trees, and a heliconia garden. Open daily from 9 A.M. to 4 P.M., except some holidays. No entrance fee.

Waimea Valley
59-864 Kamehameha Highway
Hale'iwa, Hawai'i, 96712
(808) 638-7766

Across from Waimea Beach Park on the North Shore. Plant collections include native Hawaiian plants, Polynesian introductions, and a palm garden. Open daily 9:30 A.M. to 5 P.M. except some holidays. Admission varies.

Glossary

Acidic. A pH value below 7. See pH.

Alkaline. A pH value above 7.

Crownshaft. A smooth, sometimes shiny, area that separates the trunk from the fronds in some palms.

Cultivar. A variety or form that is known only in cultivation.

Endemic. Native exclusively to one area or region. See also indigenous.

Genus. A group of related species, usually categorized by similarity or origin. The Cuban royal palm is a member of the *Roystonea* genus. Plural is genera.

Glaucous. Blue or blue-gray color on leaves covered with a waxy layer.

Indigenous. Native to an area, but can also be native to other areas.

Inflorescence. The flower stalk.

pH. In gardening, a measure of the acidity or alkalinity in the soil.

Pinnate. Used to describe feather-shaped palm leaves.

Plumose. Feather-shaped palm leaves that form on various planes, giving the frond a fuller look.

Species. A distinct entity, or type of palm, in a genus. The species name follows the genus. For example, *Roystonea regia* is the genus and species for the Cuban royal palm.

Variegated. Marked with streaks of different colors.

Acknowledgments

"What are you planning to work on next?" was the question posed to me by Jane Gillespie, production director, in the Mutual Publishing conference room. After pitching a few ideas, Jane began to envision this book.

I had been photographing Hawai'i's botanical gardens for years but had never really researched their history. While that history is now documented in this book, what's missing is a recognition of the women and men who continue to preserve and expand these botanical gardens into Hawai'i's living treasures.

Thank you, Dr. Christopher Dunn, director of the Lyon Arboretum, for your help with this project. Thanks also to Janet Leopold from National Tropical Botanical Garden and Kate Logan from Hawai'i Tropical Botanical Garden. The marketing team at Dole Plantation is outstanding; thanks to Vice President Susan Harada, Lorri Worthy, and Ephraim Botulan. Thanks also to David Orr from Waimea Valley Audubon Center.

The staff at the Honolulu Botanical Gardens is amazing, exemplified by Joshlyn Sand. Josh offered continual suggestions and photography tips.

Thanks to Terrance Leaser, Tammy and Richard Guerra, Emi Harnden, Bob Redpath, Matt Ingebrigtsen, Heidi Wulkow, and Joseph and Elizabeth Leaser. Rusty, you too.

Without the vision, talent, and support of the staff at Mutual Publishing, this story of Hawai'i's botanical gardens would remain largely unknown to many. Thanks to Bennett Hymer, publisher; Jane Gillespie, production manager; and the entire team for making this book a reality.

Finally, thanks to Paul Weissich, director emeritus of the Honolulu Botanical Gardens. If Mary Foster could be considered the mother of Hawai'i's botanical gardens, Paul is their father. Paul's vision and resolve have produced a network of gardens which is a lasting tribute to Hawai'i's early botanical pioneers, and a treasure for modern-day visitors to the Islands. Thank you, Paul.

Bibliography

Bostwick, Jeri, and Douglas Peebles. *Hawai'i is a Garden.* Honolulu, Hawai'i: Mutual Publishing, LLC. 2004.

Kepler, Angela Kay. *Hawai'i's Floral Splendor.* Hawai'i: Mutual Publishing, LLC. 1997.

——— *Trees of Hawai'i.* Honolulu, Hawai'i: University of Hawai'i Press. 1990.

Haus, Stephen Christopher. *Gardens of Hawai'i.* Honolulu, Hawai'i: Haus Associates. 2000.

Leaser, David. *Growing Palm Trees In Hawai'i And Other Tropical Climates.* Honolulu, Hawai'i: Mutual Publishing, LLC. 2007.

——— *Palm Trees: A Story in Photographs.* Los Angeles, California: Westwood Pacific Publishing. 2005.

Oslund, Clayton and Michele. *Hawaiian Gardens Are to Go To: A Treasury of Tropical Plants and Gardens.* Duluth, Minnesota: Plant Pics. 1998.

Peebles, Douglas. *Hawai'i is a Garden.* Honolulu, Hawai'i: Mutual Publishing, LLC. 2004.

Peebles, Douglas, and Leland Miyano. *A Pocket Guide to Hawai'i's Flowers.* Honolulu, Hawai'i: Mutual Publishing, LLC. 1997.

Pratt, H. Douglas. *A Pocket Guide to Hawai'i's Trees and Shrubs.* Honolulu, Hawai'i: Mutual Publishing, LLC. 1998.

Rauch, Fred, and Paul Weissich. *Plants for Tropical Landscapes: A Gardener's Guide.* Honolulu, Hawai'i: University of Hawai'i Press. 2000.

Sohmer, S.H., and R. Gustafson. *Plants and Flowers of Hawai'i.* Singapore: Les Editions du Pacifique. 1987.

Sunset. *Western Garden Book.* Menlo Park, California: Sunset Publishing Corp. 2006.

Warren, William. *The Tropical Garden.* New York, New York: Thames and Hudson, Inc. 1997.

Wood, Paul, and Ron Dahlquist. *Flowers and Plants of Hawai'i.* Honolulu, Hawai'i: Island Heritage Publishing. 2005.

——— *Tropical Trees of Hawai'i.* Honolulu, Hawai'i: Island Heritage Publishing. 2006.

Wijaya, Made. *Tropical Garden Design.* Hong Kong, China: Periplus Editions. 2004.

Index

About the Author

Award-winning author David Leaser's writing and photography have appeared in botanical journals and magazines, including *Garden Compass Magazine*, the *Palm Journal*, *Sunset*, *Islands Magazine*, and various botanical journals and newspapers. He is frequently interviewed on botanical topics by radio programs and publications, including *Garden Compass Radio*, *Garden Talk Radio*, the *Los Angeles Times*, the *Los Angeles Daily Breeze*, the *Malibu Surfside News*, and the *Sunset Western Garden Book*.

A long-time member of the International Plant Propagators Society, Mr. Leaser is in demand as a featured speaker at botanical gardens and garden centers throughout the United States, including the Los Angeles Arboretum, the San Francisco Botanical Garden, the Huntington Library, Art Collections, and Botanical Gardens; and the San Diego Zoo. He lectures on a variety of gardening and landscaping topics.

A former student at University of Hawai'i and owner of one of Hawai'i's first macadamia farms, Mr. Leaser continues to traverse the Islands photographing nature.

David Leaser received his bachelor's degree from Pepperdine University and his master's degree from the University of Southern California. He is a recipient of the Pacemaker® award for excellence in journalism.